The Purpose Living Teen

A Teen's Guide to Living Your Dreams

America's Passion Coach
Darrell "Coach D" Andrews

HYPE™, Connecting Dreams To Education™
and Passion Map™ are trademarks
of Darrell Andrews Enterprises

Darrell Andrews Enterprises
1148 Pulaski Hwy
Suite 197
Bear, DE 19701

ISBN: 0-9660103-8-8

Tele: 302-834-1040
Email: info@CoachDSpeaks.com
Web: www.CoachDSpeaks.com

Printed in the United States of America

This book is written for teenagers who want to maximize their potential in their lifetime. If you want to fully live your dreams then I encourage you to read, and study, and practice every chapter in this book! In this book I use the words "passion" and "purpose" interchangeably.

Table of Contents

Acknowledgements

It is with much joy and pleasure that I acknowledge the many people who support my work and efforts to transform the next generation though passion and purpose. I would like to thank my wife and best friend Pamela. Her constant support makes it easy to run with the vision that is inside of me. To my beautiful children, Darrell, Sophia and Alexander, thank you for loving me unconditionally; for you, I have committed my life to be an example of purpose and passion. To my mother Constance who motivated me to think outside the box, and to the many youth we have worked with in the HYPE (Helping Youth Pursue Excellence) program, I love you and believe in your dreams. I would like to acknowledge the many teachers, principals, administrators and non-profit agencies and associations we have worked with over the years. Thank you for fueling my determination to make a difference. To my friend Dr. Schuaib Meecham I say thank you for committing to the vision. To my business team of Gerry Dudley, Sheri Colt, Norma Gorham of Gorham Printing, Cathy Morgan and Linda Haskins, each one of you plays a critical role in the success of Darrell Andrews Enterprises. I am extremely proud of Mondoe Davis, an exemplary young person to say the least; I congratulate you for being selected to play football for the New York Jets and receiving your master's degree, all within a four-year period; I am honored to be your mentor.

I would also like to acknowledge George Fraser, Michelle Hoskins, Tavis Smiley, Lisa Nichols, co-author of *Chicken Soup For The African American Soul,* Dr. Jawanza Kunjufu, The Association For Supervision and Curriculum Development—in particular Kathleen Burke, Jan McCool and Marge Scherer. Further, I am indebted to Bill Milliken, Lois Gracey and Connie Walters of Communities in Schools, Inc., Superintendent Reginald James of the Gadsden County School District, Kathy Herel of the Parent Information Center, Mark Chamberlin of the Delaware Department of Education, my colleagues at NSA, James and Debbie Williams, CN8's *Your Morning* Team, *The Black Enterprise Report,* Marty Young of Foundations, Inc., and my many family members and friends throughout the USA. Thank you for believing in my gifts and talents!

Introduction

This is not your "normal" book. It is one that you will remember reading for the rest of your life. I have had the privilege of working with students all over the world, and as a result, I have subscribed to a student's motto for success: A STUDENT WITH A DREAM IS A STUDENT WITH A FUTURE. Well, actually, I did not come up with the motto, it was a theme used by the National Dropout Prevention Center for their 2004 Annual Conference. However, I think the theme is fitting for the message I am sharing in this book. *Roget's Thesaurus* lists as synonyms for dream, *a vision or a reality.* IN THIS SENSE, YOUR DREAM CAN BECOME YOUR REALITY! If you have a vision for accomplishing your dream and are willing to work diligently towards achieving it, one day you will be living it—it will become a reality. For those of you who have already put up interpersonal walls against what I am saying, let me help you. Your background does not limit your ability to live your dreams; I am living proof of that. Your family's financial situation does not have to hinder you—look at the thousands of athletes, entertainers, entrepreneurs, and other professionals who overcame poverty to ultimately experience tremendous success. The way you feel about yourself does not have to limit your possibilities. Many people started out life with low self-esteem and now see themselves in a better way. *Don't let your mind steal your dreams away from you.* Tell it what you want out of life and it has no choice but to conform. It is *your* mind, you own it, it does not or should not own you!

In this book we will strategically analyze the process of living your dreams. I say strategic because I am not writing this as a motivation book only. You need to be strategic as well as motivated. We will take a hard look at the soft skills needed to accomplish your dreams. We will consider some of the many pathways people use to find their passion in life. There is no single way to do this, so anyone who tells you so is not being truthful. We will examine the habits of passionate people, and most importantly, we will show you the path to take to remove your dreams from the canvas of your mind and place them in the reality of your existence.

It is my hope that by the end of the book you will have created a plethora of thought provoking ideas to live your dreams. Most importantly, no matter how you received the book—from a teacher, a parent, an organization, or if you purchased it on your own, please enjoy the journey. The journey is yours, and if anyone should take your journey into the future seriously, it should be you. Please e-mail me at *coachd@coachdspeaks.com* while you are on the path. Nothing motivates me more than seeing young people succeed as a result of the influence of the information in my books, tapes, speeches and workshops. I look forward to seeing you live your dreams!

Preface

Of all the books I have written, I am most excited about this one. I am starting this quest during a visit to the beautiful mountains of Reno, Nevada. When I look out of my window, I see striking snow capped mountains all around me, captivating pine trees and ravishing blue skies. It is a picture worth seeing in one's lifetime. If I were an artist I most certainly would like to capture this scene on canvas. When I think of you as a teenager in pursuit of your dream in life, I liken your life's journey to an empty canvas. Your mind is the brush that paints the picture of your life's outcomes. Your gifts and talents are the colors in the artwork by which people are amazed and captivated. **You have the ability to decide what the picture will look like; you have the ability to decide what goes on that canvas.** Just like the mountains of Reno, you will have to persevere through challenges, deal with the ups and downs and the changing seasons in your life. But just like the mountains, your life can evolve into a painting so breathtakingly beautiful that people will be astounded at what you have become. Once you identify your passion and purpose in life, and live it with vigor and determination, you become a refreshing contributor to the health, wealth and vitality of this nation. Your life becomes a valuable work of art which inspires, motivates and encourages others.

This book is for teenagers who want to make their lives count. Neither your status in life, your socioeconomic condition, nor or skin color matters. If you want to win in life and are willing to work to make it happen, you can win. I know this personally as a result of overcoming the obstacles of poverty, low self-esteem, fear, and lack of confidence. I was also raised in a family in which the majority of the people dropped out of school. Despite all of this and more, I made it. I did not end up succumbing to drugs, crime or poverty; nor did I allow people's perceptions of me to slow me down or stop me. I did not consistently permit the negative youth in my school and community to force me into making poor and destructive choices. Having my own mind, I was proud of my identity. You can be proud, focused, and determined as well. I am not saying that I was a perfect young person, however, I was focused and determined to make my life count. When I veered off the path, my inner compass set me straight again.

This book will help you to find a calling for your life, a passion to live for, a purpose for your existence. Your dreams exist for a reason. This is why I am encouraging students worldwide to go for the dream and to realize that education plays a major role in achieving them. William James, one of the greatest psychologists who ever lived stated, "The greatest discovery of my generation is that a person can change their life by changing their attitudes of mind." When you maintain the right ***attitude***, you can achieve the right ***altitude***. As Captain Kirk says on Star Trek, "You can boldly go where no man (or woman) has ever gone before." So with this in mind, we will begin the book looking at attitude's role in living your dreams. Enjoy the fantastic journey!

CHAPTER 1

Attitude's Role
In Living Your Dreams

"Attitude is the fuel that ignites the fire of passion."
—Coach D

I learned the power of attitude at a young age as a ninth grader at Roosevelt Junior High School in Syracuse, New York. Not a very confident teenager, I thought that everyone in the school was far more talented than, more athletic than, and academically superior to my meager self. I suffered from low self-esteem in the worst way imaginable.

One day, I surprised myself by trying out for the football team. Amazingly, I made the team and started the first few games; but because of my abysmally low self-esteem, I was eventually placed on the bench, never to play in another game. What I later learned was that the coach had issues, and I was randomly selected as his scapegoat. But I didn't know that at the time. So, I started to allow negative inner thoughts to dominate my mind and convinced myself that I could never succeed at anything. Then came track season, but after failure at football, I almost convinced myself that there was no way I was going to try out for the track team. Yet, momentarily telling my negative inner thoughts to take a hike, I tried out and made it! I also participated in field events, including the discus and shot put. Even though it wasn't a stellar year, I thoroughly relished the competition in track and field, and the experience increased my confidence.

The season was almost over and our coach decided to take us to the Central New York City Leagues Track and Field Championships—an event held every year for high school athletes in Syracuse. It was a highly energetic event and many junior high school students took pleasure in watching the older students compete.

I personally attended many field events the prior year, and one of particular interest to me was the discus throw. During this competition, however, something happened that changed the course of my life forever, as I watched the participants from each school warm up and prepare for the occasion. One kid especially—Matt, from Christian Brothers Academy—looked exceptionally talented...one could tell he was well coached and polished in the discus throw. I remember watching him spin and throw the discus as though it were effortless. Matt's amazing ability proved to be effective, for he not only won the competition, he broke a long-standing Central New York Cities League record, with a throw of over 156 feet. I marveled at this feat; this guy was Superman. It seemed humanly impossible, from my standpoint as a ninth grader, for anyone to ever break his record.

After a few days thinking about what I witnessed, a new boldness, courage, and passion arose in me that I never experienced before. I made a bold proclamation to myself that I would break that record by my senior year, became passionate about that goal, and set out to make it happen.

The next year, I attended Fowler High School in Syracuse, New York, and participated on the football, basketball, and track teams. Feeling much more confidently this time, I faired well in all three sports. My goal was firmly set in place: to break Matt's record; so during my junior year I became much more polished as a discus thrower, participating in the event repeatedly, as I did as a sophomore. However, I still didn't qualify for the finals—my best throw being around 126 feet. Along came senior year—last chance. I had dreamed about breaking this record for four years. This was the final opportunity, and I was passionate about seeing it come to fruition.

I was one of the best discus throwers in the county, having broken the school record of 142 feet. The goal, though, was the CNYCL record of 156 feet, 10 inches. This time, as a team, we had a stellar year; we won the Central New York Leagues Championship, ending Christian Brothers Academy's twenty-year streak of virtually unbroken championships, and I was excited that our team ended their dynasty. Passion was fixed in my mind: now was the time to compete in the meet of my life. It was my senior year, and I was the favorite to win, but nobody thought there was a realistic chance for me to break Matt's record of four years. Since my best throw was 148 feet, I wondered how I could exceed 156 feet?

With my team's support and all eyes on me, I qualified for the finals. My first throw was 154 feet—two more feet to go. My second throw was 152 feet ... backsliding. It was time for my final throw—my last chance to realize a four-year old dream. As I reflected on my dream, my passion, it seemed as though time stood still. It seemed that no one was competing against me, and the audience vanished. It was me against the world, me against my goal. Placing the discus in my hand, my extremely sweaty hand, I spun around as though my life depended on it, and let go with all my power and might. I was so emotionally attached to the throw that I couldn't watch as I let it go. All I remember hearing was a roar from the crowd. The attendant brought in the tape measure and started from the lowest number out...100, 110, 120, 130, 140, 150, 151, 2, 3, 4, 5, 6, 7, 8. When he stopped, the tape measured 158' 10". Not only had I broken the record, I smashed it!

My team picked me up and carried me off the field, my brother hugged me, my coach said he was proud of me, and in my mind, all I could think about was that an almost incredible dream had just come true. From that point until now, I believe that whatever a person is passionate about, whenever there is a desire to see it happen and a belief in one's own abilities, it can come to fruition. Who'd have ever thought that a young boy from a single-parent household with low self-esteem and lack of self-confidence could have accomplished a feat such as that? That moment changed my life forever because I realized at a young age that attitude coupled with passion equals success. It was my attitude that helped me to break that record years ago, and it is my attitude today that helps me succeed as a business owner, community leader, husband, and parent. The question you have to ask yourself as a teenager is "Do I have a positive or negative attitude about life and its possibilities?" Your attitude will determine your altitude.

Attitude's Impact On Your Life's Passion

I have coined a phrase: *the magnetic effect.* The purpose of this phrase is to help you to realize that your ability to live your calling is directly tied into your attitude. A positive attitude will attract all of the right things and all of the right resources and people, while a negative attitude will repel people, things and resources. YOU WILL NEVER SEE YOUR DREAMS COME TRUE WITH A PESSIMISTIC ATTITUDE.

Magnetic Effect:

Passionate person goes after dream
Magnet
People, resources, and knowledge follows.

When you go after your dreams with the right attitude, it's like metal attracted to a magnet—people, resources, and knowledge gravitate towards you. This effort will connect you to your destiny; your passion, coupled with the right attitude, is the power of the magnetic effect, and it works for the following reasons:

- People like to help teenagers who are doing something positive with their lives.

- Synergy comes from positive energy.

- People like to connect with others who have a vision for their lives.

The magnetic effect can also have an opposite effect:

Pessimistic Attitude
Magnet
repels resources, connections and opportunities.

As an old saying goes, "Birds of a feather flock together." Another saying goes "Misery loves company." Unfortunately, this latter saying is the category in which too many of our thoughts reside—we've been programmed by pessimism. Negative outcomes have shaped many of our perceptions in life. If our negative perceptions become our reality, we start to automatically say and do things that are negative in nature, even if we don't always completely believe them. The bottom line is that whatever attitude we choose to hold onto the majority of our time will become our comfort zone. (In a later chapter, I will share with you that I've been there and done that.) Our thoughts and associations shape our destiny. *If you as a teenager plan on living your dreams, you must design your life around a positive attitude about your possibilities.* You must also surround yourself with friends who are positive. This doesn't always mean we need a rah-rah session: you want friends who can provide you with constructive criticism, even if it's uncomfortable. You need friends who aspire to the same positive values as your own.

It's time to reconsider your relationships if you find that you and the majority of your friends are engaging in the following behaviors:

- degrading people in school, on campus or in the community;

- pointing out the negatives of school;

- discussing only the downside of living in our society;

- pointing out each other's weaknesses constantly;

- not finding anything uplifting to talk about;

- disregarding the wisdom of parents and other authority figures.

YOU WILL NEVER GET A POSITIVE RESULT OUT OF A NEGATIVE ATTITUDE. Your purpose in life is dependent upon your positive energy. Don't let negativity stop you from living your dreams.

Why Attitude Is Important

I remember reading the following quote by a Dr. Elinor Levy from of Boston University:

> *"Our thoughts affect the way we look and feel as much as even more than what we eat. Research throughout the world, including Harvard's Mind Body Institute, indicates that positive thoughts increase your white blood cell count, helping to fight disease and infection. Positive thoughts also increase your body's production of adrenaline and endorphins, which contribute to an overall vitality and excitement about life. If you want to improve the way you feel and look, begin with your attitude. Instantly feel better about yourself and your life—for less than the cost of a Big Mac."*

Attitude is important because it impacts your thoughts. YOU ARE WHAT YOU THINK. This is one of the primary factors relating to living your dreams. As Henry Ford once said, "If you think you can or if you think you can't, your right!" Mondoe Davis, the young man I mentioned in the acknowledgement section of the book, believed that he could. This is the primary reason why he will graduate with a master's degree in four years and why he was selected to play for the New York Jets. I remember first meeting him at a *How To Find Your Passion Lecture/Seminar* conducted on his campus. From the first moment I saw him, I knew that his dreams would come true. He was so passionate about making them happen that they eventually happened. On the same campus he attends, the newspaper highlights every week, students who were killed or arrested for drinking and doing drugs. Many of them fail academically or never fully reach their potential. They think that school time means party and hang out time. They are fully living out what is on their minds, having fun and not taking life seriously. Mondoe chose another path. His attitude was, "this experience is an opportunity to position myself for a good future." We all have choices, and the choice to succeed is up to you. If you are to live your dreams in this lifetime, it starts with your attitude.

ATTITUDE EXERCISE

Answer the following questions:

1. How do I feel about my future?

_____

_____

_____

2. Why do I feel this way?

_____

_____

_____

3. Do I usually think positively, or do I tend to be pessimistic?

_____

_____

_____

4. What has influenced me to think this way?

_____

_____

_____

5. If my answer was "pessimistic," what can I do starting now to change? *Examples: A. Start to listen to motivational tapes. B. Read motivational books.*

_____

_____

_____

6. What will be FIVE long-term benefits for me and for my family resulting from this change?

_____

_____

_____

7. Who can help me stay accountable to remaining optimistic?

_____

_____

_____

Chapter Conclusion

Rodger Bannister was a long distance runner many years ago when it was believed by most people that it was humanly impossible for a person to run the mile in less than four minutes. Even many physicians believed that if a person were to run that fast, his heart would malfunction. It was scientifically tested, researched and discussed by some of the greatest minds of the era. Rodger had another attitude about this seemingly impossible feat; he chose to go against the tide of popular thought. He committed himself to proving that it could be done. So Rodger went to work: he researched, studied, practiced, and inwardly convinced himself that he would be the first man to run the mile in under four minutes. One balmy day in England, a national championship track meet was held. Despite the weather conditions, Rodger was convinced that this was the day. His attitude was so positive about the possibility that many might have assumed he was being arrogant. He started the race with the pack as is customary in long distance races. At about the 800-yard mark, he broke away from the pack. With only 400 yards to go, he was clearly in charge. With all that was left in him, he made a dash for the finish line. When he broke the tape the crowd slipped into an eerie silence. Rodger Bannister ran the mile race in 3:59.4 seconds! The crowd soon exploded in applause. They could hardly comprehend what they had just witnessed. I believe that it was Rodger's attitude before the race that made this impossible feat possible.

The most amazing part of this story is what happened afterwards. Just a few weeks later, another miler ran 3:57.9 and broke Rodger's record. Soon afterwards, even *that* record was broken by yet another runner! The point I am making is that a person with the right attitude, engaged in his or her purpose can reshape history. Students, today a four-minute mile is considered slow. My question to you is: what gifts do you have inside of you that others may believe you can't accomplish? Just as Rodger Bannister did, prove them wrong. If it is truly your gift, if it is truly your passion, you can make it happen. It all depends on the attitude you possess, and the attitude you possess is unquestionably a personal choice!

Chapter 1 Key Points

List five key points that you have learned from this chapter:

1._____

2._____

3._____

4._____

5._____

CHAPTER 2

Leadership's Role
In Living Your Dreams

"What you follow decides how you will lead."

—Coach D

During my younger years, I realized that by watching other people pursue their dreams, I could ultimately achieve mine. Recognizing that people in the midst of their passions were always happy, I marveled at the exciting and wonderful lives they lived. So I started to realize this is the place where I wanted to be. This vision for my life was to cause a paradigm shift concerning my future. Having been nurtured by my mother, one of the most wonderful women on the planet—a mother of two who was a single parent with limited education—I remember as a young boy how she would constantly make encouraging statements about our future, even when it seemed as though her world was falling apart. She would repeatedly say us things such as, "You can be what you want to be in life, if you try hard enough. You need to get out and make something of your life. Don't look at what's around you here as the norm, there are people out there who are living life to the fullest, and you can too."

My mother was a people-oriented person, so she understood that this gift could help her excel in life. One day, realizing that her two boys didn't have many positive role models around to show them the way, she decided to become our role model. She went back to school and obtained her GED, pressed onward, attending business school for a year, and, as a result, was hired by USAir Inc., where she remained a valued employee in customer support areas for twenty-five years until her retirement. Despite all odds, she became passionate about our future and changed our lives forever. She pursued *her* dream, which gave us a quality of life we only dreamed about during those early years, and she still preaches the same message today as she did then: "You can accomplish your dreams in life if you just try hard enough." She was not a Rhodes scholar; however, she had as much wisdom as, if not more wisdom than any Rhodes scholar on earth. Because my mother followed her passion, I'm now able to freely live mine. She was a great example of two forms of leadership: inwardly directed and externally directed influence.

Inwardly Directed Leadership

Besides William James of Harvard University, Ralph Waldo Emerson is perhaps one of the most frequently quoted people of all times. One quote that I to which I refer to often is: "Don't go where the path may lead; instead go where there is no path and leave a trail!" This quote exemplifies what my mother accomplished and what many other people engage in—leadership from the inside out. This form of leadership states: "I am going to influence myself to do what is right and stay on the course." By far it is one of the most difficult forms of leadership. Because of the gregarious nature of teenagers, you are often moved by your relationships. Inwardly directed leadership is personal leadership which charts the course for your life. It is not driven by relationships, but is driven by a sense of identity and vision. Teenagers who realize that their lives count embrace this form of leadership, and they will not let anyone adversely alter their life's journey. They are confident and empowered. You, too, can become confident and empowered. This is a major premise of the book.

Externally Directed Leadership

This is the most prevalent form of leadership: it is leadership by association and external influence. If you plan to work in any field later in life, leadership will influence you. Even now, leadership is influencing you: your parents, friends and associates all influence you in some way. You may currently be a school leader, captain of a team, or president of a club or association. These are all forms of leadership by external influence. My mother had great leadership influence on me. Her example of determination fueled my drive to live my dream. I was inspired because she inspired me. Most importantly, I *allowed* her to inspire me. This is critical to understand as a teen on a mission: NOT ALLOWING THE RIGHT PEOPLE TO INFLUENCE YOU WILL INCREASE THE DIFFICULTY OF LIVING YOUR DREAMS. I say this because many teenagers today are turning their backs on positive forms of leadership because they don't perceive them as important. You need people to encourage you to live your dreams, but you will not live them if you don't allow the right people to mentor and assist in your life's quest. It does not matter whether your peers see it as the "cool" thing to do. It is *your* life, not theirs (Relationships will be discussed further in the next chapter.) You need to pursue both forms of leadership in order to truly live your dreams. Purpose living teens effectively employ both forms of leadership, and you need to as well if you plan to join the ranks of the passionate.

How Leaders Think

Leaders do not think like most people. I read a statistic that since 1887, 90% of the population has been following and only 10% has been leading. This is evident even in the music industry. Companies in the merchandising business have determined that you are going to in some way be influenced by the music that you love. Knowing this, they pay the entertainer millions of dollars to wear a pair of sneakers, clothing or simply a hat. They have determined that if millions of youth worldwide notice the entertainer wearing the clothing or endorsing a product, you will purchase the product. Chances are that the style of clothing you are wearing today, numerous other kids at your school and schools throughout the country are wearing also. Fads are a big part of our culture. Many teenagers are influenced, but don't even notice it.

This anecdote illustrates that leaders have goals in life and pursue their goals with tenacity and determination. Just as the music and merchandising industries have goals, you should have them. Leaders have goals for their lives and can positively influence people by assisting them in achieving those goals. Leaders are also inwardly directed. They do not need to have people telling them to work hard everyday, stay focused and committed. Such leaders are always putting aspects of life into proper perspective. If you are going to live your dreams, you must become this kind of leader: A LEADER WHO IS LED FROM THE INSIDE OUT, NOT FROM THE OUTSIDE IN. Purpose living teens are not controlled by their circumstances; they understand that they are in control of their destiny no matter what the circumstance. This is the mindset of leaders.

Exercise—Eliminating Barriers to Leadership

In order to maximize both areas of leadership, you must overcome leadership barriers. Let's take a look at some of the ways we can overcome barriers to becoming an effective leader. Take ten minutes (more if you need to), and complete the following exercises.

1. Identify areas that can hinder you from becoming an effective leader. Once identified, develop a plan of action to overcome them.

Example: Hindrance—Laziness

Plan of Action—Start to push myself daily to accomplish tasks based upon a priority list. I will eat the proper foods, get my rest, and exercise daily.

Area Identified:

Determine a plan of action:

_____

_____

_____

_____

2. Find a mentor—A mentor is someone who can help you succeed in your life's ventures.

Answer the following questions:

A. Who are four of my mentors? What two skills and/or words of wisdom am I learning from each of them?

_____

_____

_____

_____

B. Who are at least three mentors that can help me in my passion quest?

_____

_____

_____

_____

3. Surround yourself with purpose driven people—Associate with people who exhibit the following characteristics:

- ❏ positive goals for their lives;

- ❏ a determination to respect others (especially adults);

- ❏ an appreciation of sound values and standards;

- ❏ a drive for education;

- ❏ a desire to encourage me toward the positive.

Answer the following questions as you think about your four closest friends. Which of the above traits do they display? Which ones are leaders? Which ones are followers?

_____

_____

_____

By answering the questions above and developing a plan to eliminate barriers, you are well on your way to allowing leadership to help you accomplish your life dreams. This is the important second step to living your passion.

Chapter Conclusion

As a teenager, I recognized that being a leader would take me places in life. To be a leader, I felt that I needed to look like one. On the first official day on my college campus, I was determined to make a positive impression on my instructors. Noticing that most of my fellow students wore jeans and T-shirts, I decided to wear a shirt and tie. The response was much more than I could have ever expected; my professors and the staff received me very well, and even my dean wanted to know me on a first name basis. Everywhere on the campus, I was met with interest and respect by those who were employed there. One of the professors commented: "The way you look tells me where you are going in life." His words were prophetic. However, the reactions of my fellow students were quite the opposite. I heard them ask, "Where is he going, to a job interview?" "What is wrong with him?" "Who is he planning to kiss up to?" Even though their responses were negative, I realized that as a potential leader I needed to make an impression on those who could help me most. I was not there for the other students, but to create a future for myself; and the professors, career center staff, counselors and other established adults were the ones who could help me. As a result of my stand, I did become a campus leader, role model and ultimately one of the greatest success stories of the college. Leaders understand the importance of leadership when pursuing their dreams. THEY ARE NOT MOVED BY THE CROWD; THEY ARE MOVED BY THE VISION.

Because I chose to be a leader at an early age, I am reaping the benefits today. I am confident that you will stay the course of leadership so that you can carve out a commendable future for yourself. You were born to win!

Chapter 2 Key Points

List five key points that you have learned
from this chapter:

1._____

2._____

3._____

4._____

5._____

CHAPTER 3

Relationship's Role In Living Your Dreams

"Show me your friends, and I will show you your future!"

—Jim

At age eighteen, while taking a flight from Syracuse to New York City, I had an interesting conversation with a gentleman by the name of Jim, who sat next to me on the plane. He, his mother, and wife were returning home from Syracuse University where his brother had just received his degree in Political Science. Jim and I discussed everything from politics to sports. Once the plane landed, we exchanged pleasantries and were about to go our separate ways, when he asked me where I was headed; I told him that I was on my way to The Port Authority. He offered me a ride to my destination, but since I had a lot of luggage, I didn't want to inconvenience him or his family. He assured me that it wouldn't be an inconvenience to them at all. As we headed for the baggage claim area, I approached the belt to grab my luggage, and Jim asked, "What are you doing?"

"Getting my luggage," I replied calmly.

"You don't have to *carry* that." Jim looked over at a gentleman wearing a cap and directed him to pick up my luggage.

I responded timidly, "Pardon me for asking, but who's that, and where's he going with my luggage?"

Jim explained that the uniformed man with the cap was a chauffeur, and he was transporting my luggage to a limousine. We went outside, and there sat a stretch Cadillac limousine into which the gentleman placed my luggage. We entered the limousine which had everything in it, from a TV to a refrigerator. When Jim asked if I'd like anything from the refrigerator. I was so overwhelmed by the experience that I politely refused. Remember now, I was born and raised in an environment in which people only rode in limousines occasionally for funerals, but surely never *owned* one. I asked him how he came to be in a position like this because to me, it was amazing what he had accomplished at such a young age. He appeared to be only in his thirties. In turn, he began to tell me a story that had a significant effect on the rest of my life.

Jim told me of his upbringing: as a teenager, he was informed that he'd never amount to anything in life. He had several friends who were regularly in trouble; they believed that school was for wimps, and nobody took life seriously. The only future seemed to be to end up in jail or dead. So at the age of fourteen, he made a decision that changed his life forever: he decided that education was important, and life was way too serious to waste. Armed with this knowledge, he approached all of his friends and asked them to join him in his quest to do right. He said to them, "We can do this...we can achieve good grades and accomplish something significant with our lives." Of course, his friends told him he was crazy, told him to forget it; so he decided right then to let them all go. Obviously, this was difficult for him to do because he had known many of these friends all of his life. But, it had to be done.

Pursuant to this decision, he graduated from high school at the top of his class, and received a scholarship to an Ivy League school where he also excelled academically. He became an accountant on Wall Street, eventually wound up owning his own firm, and became involved in real estate ventures in lower Manhattan. Jim went from a person sure to end up in a devastating situation to one living the American Dream. He concluded his story with a key moral that helped to shape the course of my life.

"Darrell, I want to tell you something, young man, and don't you ever forget it. SHOW ME YOUR FRIENDS, AND I WILL SHOW YOU YOUR FUTURE. Because I decided to let those guys go, my life changed forever."

This was one of the most profound statements I had ever heard from a successful stranger, and I realized that my future would be determined by my decisions. The decision of friendships is, by far, one of the most critical. Please understand that I'm in no way saying that you have to cut yourself off from the world—I don't, in any way, want you to think that I'm saying that people are disposable. What I am saying is that if a person is dragging you downhill, cut the line and save your life. Don't allow anyone, or anything, to consume the energy needed to propel you towards your destination: **pursuing your life's purpose.**

What This Story Illustrates

Relationships and your dreams go hand in hand. *If you don't have the proper inner circle of friendships, you might never maximize your true potential.* In the study of great men and women on our planet, there is a common theme: the impact of the people with whom they associate. Most overachievers in life associate with other overachievers most of the time. They were/are fueled in their dreams by having people around who believed in and encouraged them to go for it. They might not have started out this way, but the sheer motivation to succeed started to draw people of a similar caliber to them. While pursuing your passion, you'll begin to locate these people, and they will find you. As you search for them, seek beyond your current database of people. Get involved and do something worthwhile with your life: volunteer at church, join local charitable organizations, or become a community or school leader. You'll immediately begin to see the impact of positive friendships result in life changes. As you give unto others, others will soon begin to give unto you. Relationships fuel your purpose in life, and they play a prodigious role in realizing your life dreams.

Creating An Inner Circle of Passion

One of the keys to establishing good relationships is a process I developed entitled :"Creating an Inner Circle of Passion". In this process you identify several people, each of whom is passionate about succeeding as a young person, excited about living a life of purpose, and motivated to accomplish personal, positive goals. And they like to associate with other like- minded people. This is important because passionate people are on a mission —they're busy fulfilling their passions and aren't standing on the roadside hitchhiking, waiting for a "hook up". In developing my inner circle, I found that passionate people are constantly on the move socially, politically, spiritually, and family-wise in many areas. Most of my wife's and my closest comrades we met through involvement with passionate activities, and the majority of them were found in church, in business, or community service. As we became involved, we found many like-minded people who've become almost like a family to us. I will even go so far as to say they *are* family. As mentioned earlier, we support one another, encourage one another, provide constructive criticism to one another, and keep each other on the straight and narrow path. We love one another and will do whatever it takes to help each other improve. We're passionate people who are simply attempting to make sure that our time spent on this planet is worthwhile. We want to bequeath a legacy of character, purpose, and passion that will be a blessing to our families and those in our sphere of influence; this is the power of having a Circle of Passion. You can help each other to press forward towards your dreams. In return, you will develop a family of friends who are a joy to be with. Additionally, you will develop the synergy needed to meaningfully run the race of life.

Developing A Circle Of Passion

As a student there are many ways to develop a circle of passion. Listed below are just three of them to help you get started.

1. Develop a study group. Associate with people who are serious about studying and doing well academically. Even if the group numbers only four or five, your combined determination will give you the strength of an army.

2. Establish a monthly motivational meeting. Meet with several people you have identified as passionate and discuss school, life and personal goals. Develop support systems to achieve your goals. Encourage and reinforce each other. Perhaps recite an "I can" mantra.

3. Develop a purpose living teen club in your school or community. The club can cover broad topics or focus on specifics relating to living your dreams. It is your choice. Please visit *www.thepurposelivingteen.com*. For information on how to start a club.

As I mentioned, this is a strategy book. Use the following form to create your plan for developing an inner circle of passion. Use the form as a way of measuring success in this endeavor.

GOAL: DEVELOPING A CIRCLE OF PASSION

Timeline:

Start Date:_____ Completion Date:_____

Action Steps:

Completion Date:_____

1._____

2._____

3._____

4._____

5._____

What/Who can help me?

Resource: *How They/It Can Help*

1._____

2._____

3._____

What are the benefits of attaining this goal?

For Self _____

_____

For Fellow Students_____

_____

For Family_____

_____

How will I reward myself? Examples—throw a pizza party; design t-shirts announcing the achievement of the circle;

_____

_____

_____

This form can be used to establish and record other goals as well. It is important to have a strategy for any endeavor. In order to develop good relationships that will help your live your dreams, you must have a strategy. Relationships can make or break you, so make it your goal to develop good friendships because too many young people are not living their dreams as a result of destructive friendships. Writing your goals make them visible and concrete. You can refer to the form often, so that you never lose sight of the vision.

Chapter Conclusion

Based upon my current goals in life, I have added key people to my Circle of Passion. I had the privilege of meeting many of these key individuals through the work I do as a speaker, consultant, and author. Most of these passionate relationships are helping me take my vision to an even higher level. IF I WERE NOT IN THE RIGHT CIRCLES, CHANCES ARE I WOULD HAVE NEVER MET THESE PEOPLE. As a student you need to realize that friendships are a critical factor in living your dreams. Keep these "don'ts" ever present in your mind:

- ❏ Do not get sidetracked by people who are trying to pull you down.

- ❏ Do not waste your days getting involved in fruitless activities.

- ❏ Do not think about impressing people who are involved in foolish, wasteful, or destructive activities.

I conclude with Jim's quote: "SHOW ME YOUR FRIENDS, AND I WILL SHOW YOU YOUR FUTURE." Please be certain to make the right friendship choices. If you are not moving forward and reaching your dreams, you're in the wrong circle. If you are alone, start your own Circle of Passion and bring friends, real friends, into it.

Chapter 3 Key Points

List five key points that you have learned
from this chapter:

1._____

2._____

3._____

4._____

5._____

CHAPTER 4

The Passion Pathways™—
Keys To Passion Discovery

"What is on the inside will ultimately manifest on the outside"

—**Coach D**

So far we have discussed important factors to living your dreams. In this chapter we will start the process of finding and living your passion. Based upon my analysis and research of living your passion one word reigns supreme: *love.* When you identify your life's purpose, you must understand one thing: if you attempt to do something that you don't love to do, even if you succeed, you'll still lose. How many people in our great nation have made it to the pinnacle of their careers and come to the realization that all the wealth, success and prosperity in the world didn't make them happy? Occasionally, a person who's in the midst of passion falls into this category as well usually because the person has no balance, is too one-sided. A balance among career, family, and activities is healthy. But (back to the statement at hand) if you ever plan to live a life of passion, unquestionably, it has to be in an area for which you have *love*.

What is love?

A famous singer once asked, "What's love got to do with it?" My response is *everything*. If love has nothing to do with it, then why do it? I understand the singer's situation because this response was probably connected to a romantic situation gone sour; however, I believe that any other motivation will become obsolete, sooner or later. People define love in many ways. Some say that love is defined as deep care for another; this is an excellent translation. Others say that love is a euphoric feeling you have for a person, place, or object, and this is also true. However, the definition that I'll give you for the purpose of this book is that "Love is the sensation you have in your heart that consumes your innermost being, and is pictured as the activity you see yourself doing for a lifetime, using your gifts and talents to make a contribution to society."

Once you get a picture of this, you're well on your way to identifying your passion. This doesn't mean that you won't have a diversified career; it does mean that your primary focus will be your passion. This chapter will assist you in doing just that: help you to identify your passion.

Many tales can be told and heard about: athletes becoming victorious despite obvious physical limitations;

artists with visual impairments who continued to perform; the man who invented the airbag, enduring years of rejection before eventually seeing his product in automobiles worldwide; singers who risked everything to simply share their musical gift. What is it that causes such fervor? What is inside these people causing them to live such amazing lives? I'm reminded of Mother Theresa who lived her whole life as a servant to others, despite the obvious inconveniences and natural discomforts. I'm quite sure that, for her, there was nothing else in the world that mattered more than serving the poor. Daily, she was living her passion, and eventually she won the Nobel Peace Prize. Then she used the prize money—all of it—to continue to serve the poor and disenchanted.

I think of my own life now as a motivator of people—a professional up-lifter. Having dreamed about this all of my life, I know it has always been my goal. I love it, and I live for it! In fact, I put so much energy into it that I dream of it at night. Seeing people maximize their gifts and talents rejuvenates me, but I abhor situations in which persons take their gifts to the grave without having fully realized them. Living my passion is exhilarating!

Recently, I was invited to speak at a business consortium on the topic "Success in Business." It was a great program, and at the end, I was invited to answer questions from aspiring business owners. One such question was, "What is the most important criterion, from your standpoint, for success in business?" My quick and immediate response was "Love." Many faces reflected confusion. Expecting this reaction, I elaborated. "You must love what you're doing, or you'll waste your time."

Most businesses fail when the only goal is making a profit, and fulfilling a passion is *not* a consideration. Those business executives see someone else succeeding in a particular venue and assume that with effort, they can achieve similar success. But they soon become discouraged and quit when they don't reap immediate benefits. They probably never asked themselves "Is this something that I really love and want to do?" Thinking about it in this way brings more validity to the statement. People who are complacent about their role as parents don't show the children the love and affection they sorely need to live healthy, productive lives. People who don't love their careers regularly spew venom to everyone around them about how much they hate their jobs.. Anything that you don't love will attract and sustain very limited amounts of your attention and won't produce much fruit in your life. Finding what you love is going to be the key to finding your passion and making a living at it.

What do I love?

This is the "million dollar" question to which most people don't have the answer. Because of this, many dreams are lost in an abyss, and will likely stay there for a lifetime, never to emerge to become reality.

Starting right now, you need to ask yourself "What's the

one thing I love that's consumed my thoughts for most, if not all, of my life?" Then, meditate on this gift and ask yourself, "Will my passion be a blessing to me and to others?" I think that it's important to point this out because the definition of passion varies from person to person. I'm not talking about passions like those of drug dealers that bring harm or devastation to the life of others, but true gifts that can positively impact lives. The majority of people achieving significance in their lifetimes have lived or are living within the realm of their passion. Make this distinction: what I *like* to do is not what I *love* to do. Likes, for me, include the following:

- Fishing

- Golfing

- Weightlifting

- Reading

- Competitive sports and activities

- Artwork

What I *love* to do is totally different. While all of these likes are wonderful, I cannot see myself doing any of these things on a full-time basis. They're not something I'm passionate about; they're simply activities that I enjoy.

Before we look at the discovery stage of this book, I think it's important to point out a few things. First, this process is rarely easy since it might be painful for you to look into your past due to the many challenges you may have experienced. It might also seem illogical that you can live your life in the realm of your dream since this is not usually the topic of conversation at the dinner table.

A second point to consider is that life has taken you on a course that's designed by your environment. For example, when I was growing up, most young African American males figured the only way to live an abundant life was by playing professional sports—I was no exception. I put everything into the sport of football, because I thought that it would eventually help me become a blessing to my mother and other family members. Because of limited environment, many of us spent years focusing our energies on activities and events that weren't the true make-up of our potential. I sometimes wonder where I would be now if I had simply focused my life on motivating and encouraging people to excellence—only God has that answer.

Therefore, we have to dig up many past experiences, desires, events, and activities to clearly see what our passions really are. I am in no way claiming that this formula is the gold standard in passion definition; I am saying that it can, and will, help you focus on the main thing that has been in your heart, the dream you seem to never shake, no matter how hard you try.

Because this is often such a challenge for many people, I have come up with five pathways that people can use to find their passion. I am confident that as a student seeking to live your dreams, one of the pathways can put you on the right path.

Passion Pathways™

Over the years I have found that there is no single way to find your passion. When I first started sharing this message I primarily used one method that I thought would work with everyone. **I was incorrect and sincerely apologize to anyone who was challenged by this methodology.** After researching, asking questions of my audience and thinking about the process in general, I identified five ways people typically find their passion and purpose in life. It is my sincere hope that this model of discovery will help in your quest to live a purpose filled life. One of the pathways "Trauma" is not the preferred method of finding it; however, many people do find it this way, unfortunately. Since it is not one that is typically relevant to students, I will not include it is this book. The remaining four pathways are:

1. Lifetime Infatuation

2. Influence of Others

3. Vision and Introspection

4. Frustration

Pathway # 1—Lifetime Infatuation

The Wright Brothers best exemplified this method. When they were little boys their father gave them a toy helicopter upon his return from a long mission. The toy helicopter gradually became their favorite toy, and they soon concluded that it was more than a toy, it had become an infatuation. They were mesmerized by it. Even though aeronautics did not exist during their time, they developed the passion to create an airplane. This passion stayed with them all of their lives. Since they couldn't shake this idea that was considered impossible during their era, they set out on a quest to reshape travel. The rest, as they say, is history. They invented the airplane, and all of us have benefited in some way from their ingenuity, whether we have taken a journey by plane or purchased fruit flown in from Brazil. This is what I mean when I say lifetime infatuation. It is something that you have dreamed of but never pursued. Your infatuation does not have to be as extensive as the Wright Brothers. You may have had an infatuation with cosmetology but gave up on it. You may been infatuated with space travel, but someone talked you out of it. Or you may have had a dream of becoming a business owner and lost the confidence to move forward. The significant point is that you still think about it. You can't seem to shake it; this is a sign that it is an infatuation, which can lead to a life's purpose.

EXERCISE

Answer the following questions to determine whether you have an infatuation with some goal. If you do not have an answer to the questions, then this method may not be for you.

1. Do you regularly dream of a career path that you are currently pursuing?

_____

_____

_____

2. Do you have an idea or invention that you can't seem to avoid thinking about? Have you wondered why no one else has ever discussed or invented it?

_____

_____

_____

3. Do you regularly tell your friends about a dream that you have even though you are not currently pursuing it? For example, have you dreamed about restoring a classic car so beautifully that you imagine people clamoring for your services to restore their cars as well?

_____

_____

_____

Based upon your responses, what infatuation do you have?

_____

_____

_____

Lifetime infatuation is a major factor in passion identi-fication for many people. However, as indicated earlier, it is not the only method.

Pathway # 2—Influence of Others

Years ago I attended a function in Chester, PA. at which the keynote speaker was Dr. Myles Munroe. From the moment he opened his mouth, I hung on to every word he spoke. He expounded upon about passion and purpose in such a powerful way that I was captivated for two full hours. One of his pervasive statements still resonates today: "Where purpose is not known, abuse is inevitable." He then went on to explain that: "Purpose is the key to fulfillment." Years later I attended another event and the speaker was the world renowned motivational speaker Zig Ziglar. Just as Dr. Munroe had captivated me with his powerful speech, Mr. Ziglar enthralled me as well. Both men influenced me in a way so powerful that I decided that I wanted also to become a motivational speaker.

Who are the people that move you? Do you get excited whenever you hear a famous artist, great speaker, business person, teacher or professor? Does your heart jump when you see animal documentaries on television? If so, this may mean that you are being influenced by an area which or individual who is in involved in your life's calling.

Many people find their passion through the influence of others. By observing others working in their field of expertise, many people become mesmerized and can see themselves in that same field. Answer the following questions to determine whether this is a method that best fits you.

EXERCISE:

1. Does your heart jump every time you see a certain individual working in a certain area of expertise?

2. Are their certain shows (cooking, art, history etc.) on television that seem to capture and keep your attention?

3. Are their certain individuals you know who have the same interests as you; and do you get excited about having conversations with this person on the topics related to the common interest?

4. What four individuals or areas of expertise seem to influence and excite you the most?

_____

_____

_____

Once again, this is a primary area of passion discovery. Hopefully it will shed some light on our life's calling.

Pathway # 3—Vision Introspection

This is the most research intensive of all of the methods. When I first started to share the message of passion, it is the one I used exclusively. To use this method, you simply start to write a journal. You record in your journal your life's activities, dreams, goals, relationships and more. The purpose of this method is to see patterns and commonalities in your life. Typically, no matter what direction a person takes in life, his or her passion keeps pulling like a magnet. As a student you may experience this regularly. YOUR DREAM IS RECOGNIZED BY PEOPLE ALL AROUND YOU. It is "in your face" constantly; however, you simply pass it off as a hobby or good thought. Yet introspection brings it to life. By journaling your life, you start to see the pathway opening wide. Some of the questions to consider in the journaling process are these

1. When your friends make the statement "you missed your calling," what is this "calling" they are referring to?

2. What activities which benefit others do you engage in naturally, effortlessly, without thinking?

3. What activities are you regularly involved in?

4. What do you love to do so much that you would do it for free?

The vision/introspection process can be a daunting way to find your passion, but it is a fun journey. If you feel as though this is method for you to use, buy a journal and start the process. Devote time to this process at least four or five times a week. It is a journey you won't soon forget.

Passion Pathway # 4—Frustration

Harriet Tubman, the slavery abolitionist best exemplifies this method. For years she was a slave in the southern plantations. But after years of toiling as a slave she grew weary living of such a meager and demeaning existence. Better yet, she became FRUSTRATED. In her frustration, she found her purpose in life: to become a Moses for slaves during the 1800's. In fulfilling her life's calling, she led more than 300 slaves to freedom by way of the Underground Railroad system. Because of her efforts and those of people such as Thomas Garret and William Still in her Circle of Passion then, many African-Americans are free to live their dreams in this country today. Thank God she became frustrated. What are you frustrated with? Are you tired of seeing you peers waste away by spending their years doing drugs and other life destroying activities? Do you dislike the way our government is currently running Social Security or Child Care services, and do you plan to become involved in politics or some type of advocacy organization to do something about it? Would you like to work to reestablish family values in this country? Are you disheartened by the way people are overwhelmed by their debt, and would you like to create a system to help people manage their money more efficiently? Many times your frustration is your passion crying out loud. It is something that you and only you were born to do in your own particular manner. Even though other people might be doing it, they will never, ever do it like you. It is your unique gift. Answer the following questions to see whether this method of passion discovery works best for you:

1. Is their something in society you want to fix?

2. Can you see yourself spending the rest of your life doing this?

3. What will be the benefit to people or to the country if you are able fix this problem?

4. How will mankind be improved by having you work on this endeavor?

Frustration is an unusual yet powerful way to find your passion. Many people have used this route, and hopefully, this method can enlighten you. So, from now on don't look at frustration as something that is only aggravating and negative. It could very well be your life's calling shouting out loud!

Advancing The Call

Did you find that one of these methods worked better for you than another? If your answer is yes, GREAT! Keep analyzing the process and attempt to bring clarity to your passion. If your answer is no, ask for help! Chances are you may need a counselor or advisor at your school to further assist you in this process. Once you are on the right path, proceed to the next chapters. IT IS IMPORTANT FOR YOU TO UNDERSTAND THE MESSAGE OF THIS CHAPTER BEFORE MOVING FORWARD. I am confident that you can do it. You were born to win! If you have found that several paths seem to overlap, narrow them down to a few you can work with. Once you are able to do this, please move forward in the book with joy and excitement. It is time to fulfill your passion!

Chapter Conclusion

Finding your passion is by far one of the important decisions you can make as a student. According to most surveys, over half of all adults in the USA dislike their current employment. They dread going to work day after day. You do not have to fall into this category. You can live a life full of purpose and passion. Hopefully one of these methods has helped to put you on the path to living your dreams. Your dream is your contribution to society. I look forward to experiencing your contribution.

Chapter 4 Key Points

*List five key points that you have learned
from this chapter:*

1._____

2._____

3._____

4._____

5._____

Purpose Empowerment— A Teenager's Strategy

"Show me a student with a dream, and I will show you a person who can make history,"

—Coach D

Finding your passion is one thing; making it happen is another. I find that this is one of the major reasons many do not live it. As a teenager, now is a good time to work on the process of identifying and living your passion, for you do not have the responsibilities of a family, house note, car note, medical insurance and all of the "fun stuff" that comes with adulthood (smile). You can go for it with enthusiasm. Many adults do not have this luxury. **The beauty of your wonderful position in life is that you have time to make it happen, without major limitations.** This chapter will help you understand the keys to making your passion a reality, once you have found it.

Passion Mapping™

Another exciting development I have included in the passion journey is the process of Passion Mapping™, which increases the options with which you can work within your passion. Once you have found your passion, there are many directions you can go take. Look at the various passion maps that follow and notice the many paths available once a person identifies their passion.

Example 1—Passion for Education

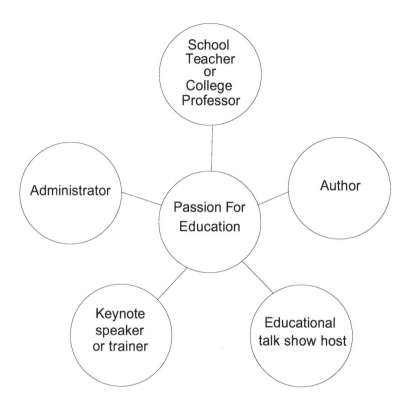

College Majors:

    1. Educational Psychology

    2. Education

    3. Educational Research

Example 2—Passion for Business

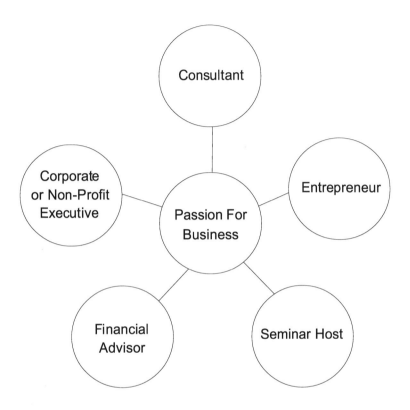

College Majors:

1. Accounting
2. Management
3. Marketing
4. Financial Management

Example 3—Passion for Sports

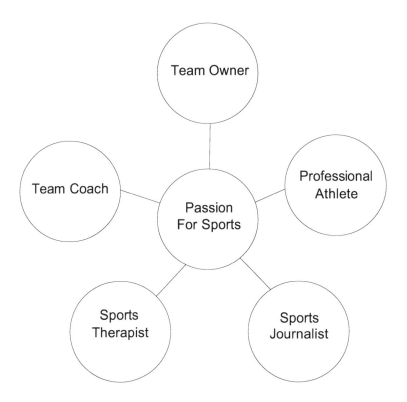

College Majors:

1. Exercise Science
2. Physical Therapy
3. Recreational Sports Management
4. Health Education

Let's create a passion map based upon your passion interest. Place your passion in the center of the circle and think about several career paths you could possibly take. Then consider what type of degrees are required in the realm of your passion.

Core Competencies—The Education Connection

Identifying the many options with a Passion Map is an exciting first step. The next step is to obtain the knowledge needed to achieve your passion. Education plays an important role once you see how it helps in your passion quest. The more knowledge you have, the greater your chance of living your dreams. Outlined below is an example of a Passion Map for the sport of football. What this illustrates is that even as an athlete, you can accomplish more with your career by gaining the necessary knowledge to succeed.

Passion—The Sport of Football

Knowledge/Competencies Needed To Succeed

- ❑ Contract Negotiation—Reading Skills, Mathematics, Writing Skills, Relationship Skills

- ❑ Oral Communications—Vocabulary Skills, Speech Communications, Conflict Resolution

- ❑ Strategic Planning—Organization Skills, Goal Setting, Logic Skills

- ❑ Athletic Ability—Motor Skills, Listening and Perception Skills, Research Skills

This information connects the importance of your current education to your future dreams. Every passion has skill sets needed in order to achieve it. By recognizing and understanding the core competencies required to live your dream, you improve your chances of achieving it.

Exercise: Please take a few moments and fill out your own passion map. Think about the possible college majors and core competencies needed to succeed.

Passion—Your Life's Purpose

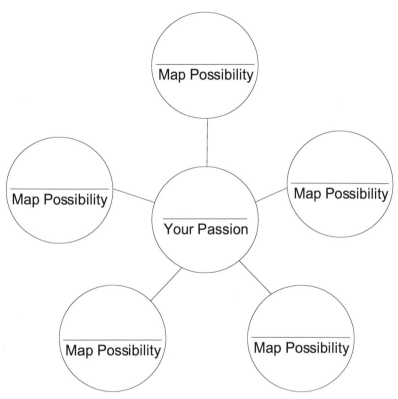

Knowledge/Competencies Needed To Succeed

❏ _____

❏ _____

❏ _____

❏ _____

Possible College Majors:

❏_____

❏_____

❏_____

By taking the time to map out your passion possibilities, you begin to recognize some of the many possibilities available to you. I began my career conducting training programs, and now I am conducting speaking programs, radio and television interviews, authoring books, creating video and audio tapes and consulting. All of my time is spent in my core area—motivation. I am simply accomplishing my passion in many ways. This is another benefit of the Passion Map: IT SHOWS YOU THAT YOU CAN OFTEN ACCOMPLISH MORE THAN ONE GOAL IN YOUR PASSION. Knowing this gives you an advantage as you map out your future. You can develop the skills necessary to maximize your life to the fullest!

Passion Organization

Dreams can come true. Your passion can make them happen. In order to assure success, however, you need to organize your life's purpose. Living in the realm of my passion was strategically planned: I organized every aspect of the vision and began to execute it point by point. Once your passion is identified, you, too, need to develop a strategy. Below is a blueprint for organizing your passion.

Passion Organization Key 1: Put in writing the vision for how you will use your passion.

A vision statement defines your passion, while a mission statement indicates what you plan to do with your passion once you've identified it.

Here is an example of a vision and mission statement.

Vision

My vision is to become one of the world's greatest karate experts. I will accomplish this by consistent study of the art, daily practice, and preparation.

Mission

From this effort, I will open schools throughout the nation that will teach people self-defense and self-discipline.

Notice how, in the vision and the mission, you see the "what and how"—what you want to accomplish and how to do it.

My Vision:

_____

_____

My Mission:

_____

_____

Passion Organization Key 2: Establish strategic goals for your passion.

It's important to look at the short and long-term aspects of your passion. While some things can happen quickly, others take more time. Establish goals for your passion, and whatever you do, be realistic—too many people try to rush things into existence. Maintain a focus and you'll accomplish more with your passion than most. In establishing your goals, you need to have *strategic* goals that are short-term (one week to one year), and long-term (one to five years). Elements of goal setting include:

- The goal itself
- A date to achieve this goal
- Strategic steps
- The resources needed to achieve this goal
- The obstacles to overcome
- A list of who can help
- An explanation of why I want to do it
- Reward

An example follows:

Goal

To improve my speaking skills. This is in line with my passion to become a motivational speaker.

Date to achieve this goal

May 1, 2006

Strategic Steps

- Join a Toastmaster's Club by June 2, 2005.

- Conduct pro-bono (free) speaking programs to polish my skills.

- Listen to one speaking tape daily.

- Practice on my own at least twice per week for two hours.

- Find a role model and mentor no later than December 2005.

Resources needed to achieve this goal

Toastmaster's Club or some other type of speaking class; NSA (spell out), or similar speech-practice organization; books on public speaking—especially those featuring the speeches of celebrated orators like Frederick Douglass, Rev. Dr. Martin Luther King, Jr., Winston Churchill, Dr. Bill Cosby., and John F. Kennedy.

Obstacles to overcome

Procrastination—I tend to put things off until later. I will overcome this by planning manageable, daily activities toward my goal.

A list of who can help

My brother (encouragement and advice);
my mentor encouragement and advice;
a speaking coach

An explanation of why I want to do it

To positively impact lives worldwide.

Reward

I will go on a shopping spree.

Your Turn

Take time to write a goal strategy for you passion.
A blank sheet is included for you to write your goals.

Goal

_____

_____

Date to achieve this goal

_____

_____

Action Steps

- _____
- _____
- _____
- _____
- _____

Resources needed to achieve this goal

_____

_____

Obstacles to overcome

_____

_____

A list of who can help

_____

_____

An explanation of why I want to do it

_____

_____

_____

_____

Reward:

_____

_____

The organization of your passion is important. *I wouldn't be making a living from my passion today had I not organized myself.* By organizing the many ways to use your passion, you focus on your target areas. By developing a vision for your passion, you shape direct future actions towards it. Setting goals is an effective way to see your vision unfold step-by-step. All of these strategies work hand-in-hand. Please ensure that you don't skip over this part because it'll make the process a lot easier if you're strategic in your approach.

Mentoring—The Passion Connection

What's the best way to observe and acquire an education, in many cases, at no cost? What's a way to shorten the learning curve? What's a way to increase the chances of success one hundred fold? *Find a mentor.* I find it helpful to compare a mentor to a parental guide: a *mentor is actually a parent of your passion.* Advice and knowledge can provide you with great insight into your future. A mentor will guide you to your destiny, correct you when you're on the wrong path, and pat you on the back when you're on the right one.

You can have several mentors in your life—a mentor for your school goals, one for your personal goals and one to help you develop the character you need. A mentor for your passion should be someone who's living your passion. As a speaker, trainer, and business owner, I have found that all of my mentors have the knowledge to assist me in achieving my dreams. If you love art, for example, find someone in that field who has the fundamental character and integrity, backed by the skills needed to provide you with advice. There are many ways to find a mentor, and we'll now discuss three of the approaches.

1. *Volunteering*

Volunteering to work at a local or national organization is an excellent way to meet a mentor. People who volunteer their time are usually people of character such as business owners, politicians, physicians, and other professionals. I volunteered for a local board concerning an annual event held in my home state. Although I wasn't compensated for my time, or even recognized for it, I was able to meet two high-profile corporate executives who gladly volunteered their time to mentor me. Their knowledge greatly enhanced my knowledge of the business-owner side of my passion. I also met an individual with years of successful consulting and training experience, and was mentored by him as well. I personally think that volunteering for an organization of your choice, and in particular, one in line with your passion, will help you to find not only one, but several mentors. As a teenager you can volunteer:

- In your school

- At your church

- For a local or national organization (perhaps a hospital, a non-profit agency

- At a local business

- For local events (state fair, benefit baseball game, health fair)

2. Networking

Another effective way of finding a mentor is networking, a key contributor to living your passion. It is also a great means by which to meet passionate, progressive people. Networking involves simply attending certain events and meeting new people who may be involved in the area of your passion. When you go, don't be intimidated by professional titles because they're human beings just like you. Keep this in mind—passionate people like to spend their time with other passionate people, so ask them questions about their careers and about themselves. Remember, people love to talk about themselves, and even if it's familiar knowledge, receive it with gladness. **As a teenager, do not be intimidated to network with adults. They realize that you are young and will respect you for having the courage to introduce yourself.**

3. Going After the Person

I read an article in *USA Today* that highlighted a very successful individual whose business beginnings were very similar to mine. Once learning the location of his business, I sent him a warm introductory letter in the hope that he would reply. Time passed, and I concluded that he wouldn't call, but my conclusion was premature. A few days later he called, and proved to be approachable and willing to share information. I drove to his facility and spent several hours learning and discussing the keys to growing a business from his perspective. He was a wealth of knowledge. So, if you meet someone who has accomplished major success in your field, attempt to connect with that person. Even if it's only a fifteen-minute conversation, it will still be worth your time. If the connection is not made, you'll be encouraged to modify your approach and try again. Mentoring is a great way to grow and develop your passion. By finding someone who's walking in the shoes you want to walk in, the process of reaching your destiny becomes easier. *Now that you have an idea of your passion area, find someone who can help you make a living at it.*

Summary

A Biblical scripture asks, "What does it profit a man to gain the whole world and lose his soul?" Many people have lived full lives only to come to the realization that they lived them in the wrong arena. They leave this earth unhappy, miserable, and conclude that they never accomplished what they always wanted to do—their true potential remained just that, potential. Don't be numbered among these people. Whatever you do, experience your passion.

As stated earlier, you have the keys to the entire world in your hands. You can decide your future, and the time is now. Take advantage of the knowledge you are learning in this text. IT COULD BE ONE OF THE MOST IMPORTANT DECISIONS OF YOUR LIFE TO DATE. Your dreams are waiting for you to capture them and make them a reality. Go for it with all that is inside of you!

Chapter 5 Key Points

List five key points that you have learned
from this chapter:

1._____

2._____

3._____

4._____

5._____

CHAPTER 6

The Habits Of Passionate People

"Your current habits will shape your future outcomes".

—Coach D.

What makes a great person great? What causes phenomenal internal and external success to come into a person's life? Why do some people seem to accomplish so much with apparently little or no effort, while others seem to struggle? *The answer lies within the internal make-up of the person: the environmental and interpersonal stimuli which that person has experienced over a lifetime, and the habits that were formed because of the stimuli.* This is my theory which I perceive it to be true. I had a cousin who unfortunately lost his life in a dreadful event. Several years prior to his death, he posed a dilemma which still haunts me: "I want to change, but I just don't know how to." At the time, I was very young and didn't have a meaningful response for him. Because of the negative environmental stimuli in his life, he formed bad habits that unfortunately led to his demise. I loved my cousin and mourned his passing; therefore I sometimes wish he were around now, so that I could give him better advice.

A habit is defined in Merriam Webster's Collegiate Dictionary as a "usual manner of behavior;…an acquired mode of behavior that has become nearly or completely involuntary". Habits can make or break a person. Millionaires are rich because of habits, and drug addicts are dependent because of habits. Students earn good grades because of habits. Parents are primarily effective or ineffective because of habits.

Habits can make or break a person. Millionaires are rich because of habits, drug addicts are addicted because of habits, students receive good grades because of habits, and parents are good or bad parents because of habits. A habit is defined by Roget's Thesaurus as an "activity done without thinking," or "a habitual way of living."

How are habits formed?

Repeatedly performing a certain activity over an extended primarily forms a habit. The psyche becomes adjusted to this particular behavior, so that it becomes the norm. Business people who have developed sound business practices will most often have successful businesses. By contrast, business owners who develop poor habits or have no habits typically go bankrupt very quickly. Kids born into impoverished situations typically take on the habits of their environment and reproduce them in their own lives. The corollary is that children born into loving households take on the characteristics of those households, and duplicate them in their own lives.

In order to form good habits, you must practice doing positive things. When I was younger, I developed the habit of saying what I *couldn't* do, so my mother corrected this negative affirmation by instructing me to say what I *could* do. I'm so glad that she did because it has made all the difference in my life. She assisted me in developing habits that have shaped the course of my life in a most positive way. In this chapter, we're going to look at the habits of passionate people, and how they are able to use these habits to shape their destiny.

The five habits we'll take a look at are:

Habitually speaking positively
The habit of speaking positively about
your progress and potential;

Being actively involved
The habit of becoming involved
with activities that propel your passion;

Asking "What are you thinking?"
The habit of overcoming negative thoughts
with positive ones;

Saying "Oh, no!"
The habit of saying "no" to activities
that will take you off course;

Visualization
The habit of thinking into the future,
despite the current situation;

Habit 1: Habitually speaking positively

In our training program, HYPE (Helping Youth Pursue Excellence), we have a training module called *The Seed of Your Words* designed to illustrate the power of words. Using a "call and response" pattern, we begin by saying some common words like "pizza," to which the trainees respond, "good," "tasty," "delicious," or "would like some now." Then we say a word such as "homework." We are given different, usually negative responses such as, "hard," "boring," "cuts into my play-station time," or "a pain." Following that, we ask, "Why is it that when you heard the word 'pizza,' you gave us a positive response, and then when we said, 'homework,' you gave us a negative one?" After a brief discussion, we explain that both words impacted their internal thought system in some way to produce a response. The words themselves were a stimulus. I believe that most words have what I call "impact-ability"; they have the power to impact you positively or negatively. Words can be felt. Just as the training module states, "Words are seeds," the seeds go into the soil of your heart, and with the help of more words, continue to grow. Bottom line: what you say can make or break your passion.

Purpose-living teens talk about themselves and other things in an uplifting manner, instead of in a derogatory one. They live in the positive realm, so with this in mind, the first habit of passionate people is the habit of speaking positively about their potential.

As a child, I constantly whined, "I can't." It didn't matter what the task was, I automatically said it. My mother would tell me, "Son, don't say you can't; say you can." For years we went back and forth. I would say "I can't," and she'd respond, "You *can*." Eventually, her continued persistence paid off, and I began to automatically say, "I can." It didn't matter how I felt inside, outside, or any side—I came to believe what my mother told me. This attitude has been a great foundation for success in my life, an attitude that's helped me as an athlete, student, father, and a husband. I never let obstacles stop me in any way, because I believe in my potential. Words are the fuel for our motives; what we say is what we become. This is why I love being a motivator. My words can motivate a person to go for goals in life.

What you say about yourself is a direct indicator of what's inside of you**.** *In order for your passion to take full form, it needs your cooperation*. Think about yourself for a moment and then answer the following questions:

- How do I feel about myself?
  Why do I feel this way?

- What words do I use to describe myself
  and why?

- What are my five most important values?
  Where did they come from?

- What are my five highest standards?
  Where did they come from?

- What do I watch most often on television
  or listen to frequently on the radio?
  What am I allowing to penetrate my mind?

The answers to these questions will provide insight into the influence of words in your life. Passionate teenagers decide the words that go into their lives instead of allowing those words to simply slip into their subconscious mind. From this point forward, think about everything that goes into you mind, and realize that these words are shaping your perception of life. Take control of words, and you can literally write your future.

Words and our environment

In some of our training classes, we conduct an unusual exercise: we ask people to lift their hands slowly and then lift them quickly; we ask them to sit up and then sit down; we ask them to smile and then frown. When we complete all of the activities, we ask, "Why do you think we did this exercise?" We obtain a variety of responses, but never do we hear the one we're looking for, so we explain that the reason for this exercise is to show them how much they're in control. We gave them a stimulus (a command) and they responded—they made the decision to respond to the stimulus; nobody made them do it. The concept we're really trying to teach is that since you're in control, you can, by the use of appropriate words coupled with corresponding actions, direct yourself along the path you want to go. Many students don't realize this until it's pointed out. The majority of lives are spent under the influence of the opinions and words of others—values, standards, opinions, activities, and habits have been hand-delivered by our friendships with other people. Many have never considered self-direction.

If you're going to be a teenager of destiny and passion, you *must* take charge of your own life. Understand that you cannot progress if you continue down the same path and regularly associate with people who lack passion. If you want to be a person of passion, you must change your environment: you need to re-focus. The wrong environment, associating with people, places, and things that send the wrong message can be devastating. Negative words that come from this environment can have a damaging effect.

Along with your own words, the words of others can a have significant impact on your life. In my first year of returning to college, I started to associate with people who wanted to do everything except acquire an education. Their only mission was to party, hang out, and enjoy their newfound freedoms. Based upon my previous college experience, you'd have thought I knew better, but I began to hang around a certain group because the words that they used to keep me in that group were compelling. The guilt trips they tried to send me on and their attempts to force me to show compassion for their ways—the crab technique—kept me in the basket.

Then one night, that "I can't" whine echoed; then ever so faintly, but persistently, I heard "Yes, you can." I would have ignored it, but numbers started flashing through my mind 110, 120, 130, 138, 142, 158....memories of my discus throw enveloped me like a heated blanket on a bitterly cold winter's night. The bedraggled reflection I had seen in the mirror the morning before was replaced by the image of a clean-shaven young man in a shirt and tie. Even though I had allowed my passion to be dragged down into the abyss, it was indefatigable, and I felt it propelling me forward again. Before dawn the next day, I decided that enough was enough, and broke off the negative friendships. They harassed me for months afterward, but I found a new set of friends who were serious about their future, and these relationships meant much more than the ones I had with the previous group. Most importantly, our conversations were uplifting and motivating, unlike those in the previous relationships. Most of my newfound friends soon graduated from college, whereas the most in the previous group failed or dropped out of college. Besides the activities in which we participated, the greatest difference between the two groups was the communication established in the latter group: we encouraged each other, and this made a world of difference.

You can be heavily influenced by other people, whether you like it or not. Since this is often the case, it becomes increasingly more important to control and take charge of your environment; otherwise, it will be extremely difficult to live your passion. Remember, your friendships will inevitably influence the words you say about yourself; so whatever you do, think about whom you are around on a regular basis and make positive changes, if necessary. Your associations will definitely impact the words and attitudes you internalize.

Habit 2: Being actively involved

As time passed, I succeeded in the corporate world, but I lacked a love for what I was doing. So I resigned from Abbott Laboratories and established my own business. Initially, I couldn't understand it. I had a good message, was well prepared, and still had no business. "It just doesn't make sense," I used to say. My wife and I began examine more closely what we were doing and considering what we were perhaps failing to do. We asked around, sought advice, and eventually came to a common-sense answer: most people who were landing business contracts knew other people who referred prospective clients to them—simple, but true. Having a good product, excellent service, and choice location doesn't guarantee success. What many fail to realize is that to the extent that you serve the community, the community will serve you. The bottom line: you simply must become involved. The more involved you are, the more people you'll meet, and the better your chances of success. Prior to this revelation, I neither had an idea what a board of directors was, nor what its purpose was. Now I am a member of quite a few boards, and I chair several of them. I genuinely enjoy what I do. Many people now know what my business offers and regularly refer my services. If I hadn't become involved, this would never have happened. Don't get me wrong; I'm not telling you to become involved solely for reciprocity. I'm saying that it's a good way to share your passion with a multitude of people, as well as serving your community at the same time. Passionate people want to be heard. They realize that it takes people to make their passion a reality. *Teenagers who get involved typically accomplish more in life than those who don't.*

Everything we do in life is, in some way, connected to other people. If you desire to be a scientist, your science can be a blessing to the nation. If you desire to be a singer, your voice can motivate and comfort many. If your love is banking, your financial knowledge will help people to establish a secure financial future. If you desire to be a law-enforcement officer, you can protect people from harm and danger by providing a secure environment for all. No matter what your passion is, it can positively impact the lives of others. This is why it's key for others to know about you and your passion. Simply keeping it to yourself isn't going to do anything for anyone. You need to get out, be involved, and let the world know about your dream. Get involved now! Don't wait until all your "ducks are in a row" (that is to say, until everything is perfectly set in place.) There will never be a more perfect time than *now*. Start attending local events relevant to your passion. Keep one thing in mind: *becoming involved doesn't mean giving up all of your time* (see section on, Oh, No!); it simply means keeping connected to individuals and activities that can help push your passion forward. Here's an example of how to become involved:

Passion
Dancing. I'd like to be a choreographer.

Goal
I want Accomplish this within a two-year period. Organizations and activities in which I could become involved:

I can volunteer to assist in a local dance class or volunteer to develop a stage play that includes choreography.

I'll make it a point to attend three or four local dance programs each month, and become acquainted with the key people. Obtaining an apprenticeship is a possibility.

Being involved gives you energy and encourages you to go for the gold medal, so to speak. Just sitting around only promotes frustration and a sense of hopelessness. Your dream is only beneficial if you add the dimension of *action*. Purpose-living teens are constantly on the move. They're involved and striving to achieve and contribute on a daily basis.

Habit 3: What are you thinking?

One of the hardest areas to perfect in my life was my "thought life." Yes, along with the life that you physically see, you have what's called a "thought life." In this life, mental images, environmental stimuli, and interpersonal stimuli play key roles in shaping what will manifest in your outer life. For me, this was a huge challenge, because I was trying to create a lot of "firsts" in my family: the first to receive a bachelor's degree from college; the first to hold a corporate-level position; and the first to successfully become an entrepreneur. My negative inner thoughts were having a field day because I had no closely connected models of success to whom I could refer. Many times, I fell into mental despair. Oftentimes I felt overwhelmed, and occasionally still feel that way. Being the first at anything is hard, *but a passionate person won't allow negative inner thoughts to rule. Be persistent.*

The mind is made up of a confluence of will, emotions, intellect, soul, and spirit. Your goal should be to develop a level of balance that will allow you to think clearly and achieve whatever dreams you have in life. Most of us weren't born into perfect situations, so we're usually off balance in some way. We're constantly calibrating our lives, and this makes advancement tough. Most of this readjustment is a result of our thought life.

By taking control of your thoughts—plain and simple—you take control of your life. In order to live your passion, you *must* exercise self-control, or you won't make it. Your thoughts must be clear, concise, and positively charged—not bogged down with useless and destructive negative images. You *must begin to make your mind agree with the paths that you have chosen to take and reverse the lifelong curse of negativity that you may have been dealt.* Passionate people have mastered this art. *Even though their minds might not fully incorporate positive thinking, the mind complies with what it is given.* As a passionate teenager, you can turn positive thinking into a habit so that this pattern starts to impact every area of your life, and in many ways begins to spill over into the lives of others. You will begin to see things in a way that you've never considered before. You become a positive magnet (magnetic effect).

Listed below are four keys to establishing the habit of positive thinking that will propel your passion:

- Listen to motivational tapes daily—start to fill your mind with positive affirmations.

- Find two or three students who think like you,

and form an inner circle—these are friends you can always depend on to provide you with motivational feedback, particularly if it's constructive criticism.

- Tell your mind to be still regularly—don't let negative thoughts win; tell them to leave your mind (not openly in public—we don't want you to frighten others who may think you're arguing with yourself—but privately, to yourself). Remember, you don't have to say a word to your subconscious; you can simply think a positive thought to erase the negative thought.

- Read one good inspirational book per month—this is another way to flood your mind with positive messages.

It's important for you to remember that you are who you are due to a lifetime of circumstances. In order to change the way you think and pursue your passion, you need to make a determined effort to reinforce positive thoughts. The way you think is a sure sign of your future success, so start to train your mind now—your present and future success in life depend upon it.

Habit 4: Oh, no!

My son's vocabulary was excellent for a two-year-old, but one word he mastered more than others was "No." I'd ask him to do something, and with a determined expression on his face, he'd look at me and say, "Nnnnooo," —drawing it out for masterful effect. I'd ask him repeatedly, but I would only hear, "Nnnnnoooo." Naturally, Daddy had to correct this behavior at some point; however, my son was determined to stand his ground, and his opinion was unwavering: he was defending what he believed. As a purpose-living teen, you must know when to say, "No." Even though we recommend becoming involved, please acknowledge that you cannot do everything—a sense of realism must be in place.

There was a time when I simply had too much activity in my life. I was trying to help everyone, assisting where and when I could, *and* maintaining my own personal life. I began to feel overwhelmed, and within a few years, my productivity took a nosedive. I had a major problem: I just couldn't say, "No," to people. Constantly, I was approached for assistance of one sort or another, and my invariable response was, "Yes." This left me with little time to pursue my dream in life.

Saying, "No," to people who are accustomed to hearing, "Yes," all the time is a very difficult process. If you have an amiable disposition, it is *extremely* challenging. When you work on your passion, a higher value is placed on time because there is not an inexhaustible supply of it; thus, it becomes impossible to do *everything*. When pursuing our passions, we must realize that time is one of our most effective tools, so we must become comfortable saying, "No." Start doing this immediately. Practice it this week. When you feel the urge to say, "Yes," say to the person in a diplomatic way, "I'm sorry, but due to my schedule, I must say no." Once you make this statement, stand on it, and don't deviate by allowing your mind to be persuaded by someone else. My wife often reminds me: "When you have a compelling yes on your mind, 'No,' becomes easier to say." Your compelling yes should be your newfound passion by which you want to make a successful life. Don't compromise this for anything.

Habit 5: Visualize

Living in poverty can actually be beneficial in some ways. Attending an event in Delaware, I heard keynote speaker making a statement that was shocking to me. He was raised in poverty and had to work hard to accomplish his success in life. Jokingly, he said, "My kids are the ones who should be considered handicapped, due to the fact that they don't have to work hard for anything. They don't understand hard work, so in many ways, this can be a disadvantage." What an interesting viewpoint. The greatest thing about starting from the bottom is your ability to form a mental picture regarding what you want to accomplish. There is no natural relationship with your dream except the one that's in your mind. You have no friends who have experienced this particular dream, and every aspect of your dream unfolds one event at a time. You *visualize* the end with no natural means or understanding about how it's going to happen but believing that it will. By diligently working at it every day, one day you eventually will accomplish exactly what you set out to do.

Visualizing, simply put, is the habit of forming a subconscious picture of your vision and mediating upon it. This act of passion has been one of the sole reasons for the tremendous success of millions of people worldwide: individuals, businesses, and organizations build their futures based upon visions. By meditating on your vision, your entire being begins to accept the fact that this is more than just an idea or a good thought: this is something that will someday become a reality. Even Biblically we are encouraged to act on a prayer request as if it were already answered. Speak those things which are not as if they were so. I heard one actor say he wrote a check for ten million dollars and dated it three years into the future. He said he'd be able to cash the check at that time, and sure enough, precisely three years later, he cashed it!

I recently spoke to a girl's field-hockey team about winning their conference championship; this team wasn't expected to win the championship or even rank as a major contender. My staff and I conducted a visualization exercise in which the team *saw* themselves celebrating the championship. They were extremely motivated and began to believe that they could actually do it. What do you think happened? They made it all the way to the championship game but lost by only a few points. *Keep in mind, they weren't even expected to be contenders for this coveted prize.* Their coach recently contacted me and said, "Your speech was the foundation to the success of their season."

In their minds they had a unified picture which became their driving force. One of their assistant coaches told me that after my speech and recommendations, they became more competitive in practice, they supported each other more intensely, and were more open to share ideas. They saw something that day that served as a paradigm for their potential. Hopefully, athletes will also use this technique to conquer other challenges in life.

The Power of Sight

All my life I've visualized. Prior to my corporate sales experience, I was impressed by seeing sales representatives drive around in their company cars, wearing their chic suits, negotiating on their top-of-the-line cell phones, and from that I realized there were different levels of sales. Of course, I wanted to be in one of the key sales fields, so after thorough research, I decided that I wanted to work in the medical sales field. I even knew what company I wanted to work for—Abbott Laboratories. Thus, I began to visualize myself being a top-rated salesperson for Abbott, building my customer base. At the time of this visualization, the medical sales field was primarily interested in hiring people who held degrees in such life sciences as sociology and biology. Realistically, since I had a degree in business, I shouldn't have been in contention to work for any medical firm, let alone a major one like Abbott. The recruiter who was working for me told me that I'd need to acquire a few years of experience before even *considering* entering the field. He assured me that there was no way that a company in the medical field would hire me because I lacked the proper credentials. However, I told him to continue to pursue such opportunities anyway, and I would deliver when the time came. You see, this was my passion pathway. He agreed, and continued to seek employment opportunities for me. Soon thereafter, I received a phone call from him stating that he had an unbelievable opportunity for me, although he was sure I wasn't ready for it. Nevertheless, he thought an interview was warranted, even if it turned out to simply be practice. "Don't expect in any way to get the job; just use it as a time to get an understanding of the process," he warned.

I probed him for information about the opportunity, and finally persuaded him to tell me the location of the company. The moment he revealed the location, I knew it was Abbott. After confirming it, I proceeded to relate my vision for working with this company. I had a vision to work there, and no one or nothing was going to deny me this position because this was not merely a coincidence, but a destiny. Having already studied the company, their competition, products and services, divisions, and sales representative expectations, I was ready and determined—preparation finally met opportunity. "I respect your enthusiasm, however, this is no ordinary company," the recruiter replied. "You won't get this job, but let's give it a try."

I arrived at my interview prepared, positive, and determined. The district manager who interviewed me was stern and straightforward: she was a former army captain and demonstrated military mannerisms during the interview. She was respectful, but direct and firm, asking me extremely difficult questions, ones which I was prepared to answer. My vision was clearly illustrated in my mind, and I was determined to show her that I was the man for the job. At the end of her interrogation, she asked me if I had any questions for *her*. I replied, "Yes, I do." My next move was a major surprise, even to me, but I realized this was the only chance to give it my all. "How's the interview process coming along?" I asked.

"It's been tough; I've over one hundred resumes, and many more forthcoming," she sighed.

"I guess this must be somewhat of a demanding process for you," I responded.

"Yes, it is," she replied wearily.

"Well, I have a solution to finalize the process for you. I see that stack of resumes on your desk, and I also notice that you have a trash can next to it My recommendation is that you take the resumes and dispose of them in the trash can. You don't have to look any further because the best person for the position is sitting right here before you!"

She looked at me in amazement. For about thirty seconds she simply stared at me, then got up, strode to the regional manager's office, and I believe, said to him, "Our man's sitting in the next room." Within a week, I was an employee of the company—the process normally takes a lot longer. **I believe, to this day, that the only reason this**

happened the way it did, was because of the passionate vision that I had for the position. I refused to be denied, and this allowed all things to come together for my good. That job turned my life around, giving me an experience I'll never forget. *Having a vision can make the impossible seem possible. All it takes is a clear focus on what you want, thinking about it, and putting those thoughts into action.*

Keys to Effective Visualization

Below are six keys to effective visualization which will guide you on your path to creating a clear picture, and soon, to the manifestation of your passion.

1. Do not eat anything sweet, or drink anything with caffeine before visualizing. Your mind needs to be totally relaxed, not in high gear.

2. Find a quiet place (e.g., home or local library) where you can sit and relax. This area must be disturbance and distraction free—no chatty friends, no music, no radio, no television.

3. Create a vivid picture in your mind which reflects the goal you want to accomplish, and develop it into a "dream movie" of which you are the producer, director, and star.
Look at the goal from every angle you can imagine. For instance, if your passion is to become an architect, think about designing a building. See yourself in a

room with all of the blueprints scattered around you, then going to the site and consulting with all of the contractors. Think about the various stages of the building process, and see them developing right before your eyes. See your building as part of the majestic skyline in one of the world's major cities. Think about the completion of the building, the ribbon cutting ceremony by the governor (or the President). It's your dream movie, so have fun. Enter the building and visually inspect all of the offices: look at the work of your hands. Read a few newspaper articles about your magnificently completed project. What wonderful comments are they writing about your accomplishment? See yourself winning awards for your awesome facilities. What are you going to say at your awards banquets? Then, open your eyes and reflect on your vision.

4. Using pen and paper, to write down any pertinent information you received as a result of this vision.
If it's something that you can act on, begin to act on it now. For example, if you're at the library, borrow books relating to the vision. Develop a vision poster with pictures of various aspects of the vision. Place the poster on your bedroom wall.

5. Do this at least once a day for about 20-30 minutes.
The more frequently you do it, the more you will begin to see the manifestation of your dream.

6. Enjoy the vision.

Every great action or activity started as a vision in a person's mind and resulted in a blessing to our society. Your vision can do the same.

Make these keys a daily habit. Compelling your mind to believe in your passion requires dedication: remember that your passion's been there for years, but your subconscious prohibited you from moving forward. By spending time visualizing, the inner determination will become an outer reality.

Summary

Not all habits are bad. As a teenager in pursuit of your dream, it is important to understand this. In this final chapter, we wanted to focus on the habits that cause passionate people to accomplish a life of their dreams. If you've developed bad habits during your lifetime, with diligence, you can reshape them into *good* habits. Your habits directly correlate with your future. If you're going to do anything on a consistent basis, make sure it's something that will propel you forward. Passionate people decide their habits—they're in control of themselves, and therefore, of their future. Make it a priority to establish these positive habits in your life; you success will cause you to be thankful that you did. Most importantly, connecting with other young people who have developed positive habits as well will make it easier to stay on the path to success.

Closing Remarks

Your future is too important for you to ignore. Understand that you can and will live your passion. You don't have to be afraid of it or believe that it can only happen to someone else. You now have the formula for success.

This book is my contribution to teenagers worldwide, because I believe that you count, and are important to mankind. People aren't born bad; but life can turn them into bad people. People aren't born angry and insensitive; however, unfortunate circumstances can turn them that way. People who are born poor don't have to remain that way. People who are born with a physical, mental, or emotional disability, can still make the most of life. We can help each other.

Life, in most cases, is about choices, and those choices we make create our future. Our future indicates our legacies. Choose to live life to the fullest, and remember one thing: never ever give up. If you use the information shared in this book by doing something tangible with it, you'll live your passion and begin to realize the dreams inside you. Your life will say to the world, "I'm here, and I *do* make a refreshing difference."

You now have no excuses. You can now propel yourself forward with everything inside of you. You now know that YOUR CURRENT EDUCATION IS NECESSARY FOR YOUR FUTURE DREAMS. Take every class seriously, knowing that the more wisdom and knowledge you acquire, the more options you will have in life. Go to class with this new found meaning at hand, focus, and excel.

Because you read this book and applied its contents, I know some day we'll meet in the land of the passionate. Only a few people in every generation arrive in this wonderful place, but I look forward to your name being included in the HALL OF PASSION! God bless you, and HAVE A PASSIONATE DAY.

Chapter 6 Key Points

List five key points that you have learned
from this chapter:

1._____

2._____

3._____

4._____

5._____

About The Author

Darrell "Coach D" Andrews, president of Darrell Andrews Enterprises and FamQuest, Inc. His other books include; *How To Find Your Passion And Make A Living At It, Believing the Hype—Seven Keys to Motivating Students of Color, and Believing the Hype.* He is also the developer of the *HYPE (Helping Youth Pursue Excellence) School of Dreams Video Series.* **Coach D is a highly sought after motivational speaker, trainer and consultant.** He regularly speaks at conferences and events throughout the United States on the topics of passion, positive attitude, youth motivation and professional development.

Not allowing childhood challenges to stop him, Darrell's passion walk began early in life. As the son of a high school dropout and a single mother on welfare, he became a three-sport all-star in high school, a leader at his college and the first college graduate in his family. This is amazing, considering that when he arrived on his college campus, he was neither registered to attend, nor did he have the money to pay tuition. Yet his passion for more out of life compelled him to pack everything he owned into five garbage bags and hop on the bus to a city where he had never been with a one-way ticket and $42 dollars in his pocket. Reflecting on the experience, Darrell states, "I didn't know where I was going, but it had to be better than where I was."

Regularly, he appears as a guest on numerous radio and television programs locally and nationally. Darrell has been interviewed on NPR Radio's *Tavis Smiley Show,*and is known as "America's Passion Coach" on CN8's *Your Morning,* and has been featured in *Black Enterprise* magazine. He is the recipient of many leadership awards, including the Philadelphia "40 Under 40" Minority Executive Award.

He has received mayoral proclamations for the development of the Youth REACH Leadership Council and for being a positive role model to the youth of Wilmington, Delaware. As a community leader, he serves on a number of community-based boards of directors. Coach D's HYPE "Helping Youth Pursue Excellence" program has received accolades from organizations throughout the USA. Coach D holds a Bachelor of Science degree in Business Administration from Cheyney University in Pennsylvania.

He and his wife Pamela are blessed with three marvelous children.

Order Form

MAIL THIS FORM AND PAYMENT TO:

Darrell Andrews Enterprises, Inc.
1148 Pulaski Hwy., Suite 197
Bear, DE 19701
or fax this form to: (302) 832-6127

SHIP TO:

_____
NAME

_____
ADDRESS

_____
CITY   STATE   ZIP

_____
TELEPHONE   EMAIL

The Purpose Living Teen	$12.95	
The Purpose Living Teen's Student Guide	$20.00	
The Purpose Living Teen's Workshop Facilitator's Guide	$49.95	
How To Find Your Passion And Make A Living At It (ISBN 0-9660103-3-7)	$12.95	
Believing The HYPE: 7 Keys to Motivating Students of Color (ISBN 0-9660103-5-3)	$12.95	
HYPE School of Dreams (ISBN 0-9660103-7-x)	$149.95	
Chicken Soup for the African American Soul (ISBN: 0-7573-0142-8)	$14.95	
	SUBTOTAL	
Add 30% of product total for shipping charges	SHIPPING	
	TOTAL	

PAYMENT INFORMATION:

☐ Check or Money Order (Payable to Darrell Andrews Enterprises, Inc.)

☐ Bill my credit card # _____

   ☐ Visa   ☐ MC   ☐ AmEx   Exp. Date_____

   Signature_____

☐ Purchase Order #_____

Please allow 4 to 6 weeks for US delivery.
Prices are subject to change without notice.